P9-CCB-411

EVERYDAY HANDBOOKS

FIRST BOOK OF
CHESS

by AL HOROWITZ *and* FRED REINFELD

the text of this book is printed
on 100% recycled paper

BARNES & NOBLE BOOKS

A DIVISION OF HARPER & ROW, PUBLISHERS

New York, Evanston, San Francisco, London

TABLE OF CONTENTS

©

FIRST BOOK OF CHESS

Copyright, 1952, by Sterling Publishing Co., Inc.

LET'S PLAY CHESS

Copyright, 1950, by the Editors of *Chess Review*

All rights reserved under International and

Pan-American Copyright Conventions

Reprinted by BARNES & NOBLE, Inc.

By special arrangement with Sterling Publishing Co., Inc.

L. C. Catalogue card number: 53-6456

SBN 389 00225 9

Manufactured in the United States of America

1   *The Chessboard*

2   *The Opening Position*

THE ELEMENTS

CHESS is played by two opponents who move alternately.

The game is played on a *chessboard*. This board is made up of eight horizontal rows and eight vertical rows of eight squares each. (*See Diagram 1.*)

The squares are alternately light and dark. This makes it easy to distinguish adjacent squares from each other. Unlike checkers, chess calls for the use of *all 64 squares.*

As the game begins, each player is provided with 16 chessmen. Again, for the sake of visual clarity, it is conventional to have 16 light-colored chessmen and 16 dark-colored.

The light squares are always referred to as *white squares;* the dark squares are always called *black squares.*

Similarly, the light chessmen are the *White pieces,* and the dark chessmen are the *Black pieces.*

The player who has the White pieces is known as *White;* the player of the Black pieces is referred to as *Black.*

As the game begins, each player has the following forces:

WHITE			BLACK	
	one	KING		
	one	QUEEN		
	two	ROOKS		
	two	BISHOPS		
	two	KNIGHTS		
	eight	PAWNS		

Each player sets up his pieces* in a standard formation on the two rows nearest him. (*See Diagram 2 and the photograph at the top of the next page.*)

---

* The term *pieces* is used interchangeably for all the chessmen, or for any chessman other than the Pawns.

The Opening Position

Diagrams are extremely helpful to you in your reading of this text. You will therefore find it worthwhile to compare each piece in your set (or in the photograph) with its corresponding symbol in the diagrams.

Remember that in all diagrams, *White's* side is always at the *bottom; Black's* side always at the *top*. White moves *up* the diagram; Black moves *down* the diagram.

When setting up the pieces to begin a game, always make sure that the player of White has *a white square in the right-hand corner nearest to him*.

Inexperienced players sometime make the mistake of transposing their King and Queen at the beginning of a game. There is a simple rule that will help you: *Queen on color*. The White Queen goes on a white square, the Black Queen on a black square, and they face each other along the same vertical row. Note that the two Kings also face each other along an adjacent vertical row.*

The Bishop next to the King is known as the *King Bishop*. The adjacent Knight is the *King Knight*. The Rook in the adjoining corner square is the *King Rook*.

Similarly, the three pieces next to the Queen are the *Queen Bishop, Queen Knight* and *Queen Rook*.

This gives us the names of the Pawns. The Pawn in front of the King is the *King Pawn;* the Pawn in front of the King Rook is the King Rook Pawn, etc. Can you name all the Pawns?

The first move is always made by White After Black replies, White makes his second move, which is in turn answered by Black; and so the game continues with alternate moves.

---

* These vertical rows are called *files*. The file on which the Queens stand is the *Queen file;* the file on which the Kings stand is the *King file*. The other six files are likewise named after the pieces which stand on them at the beginning of the game.

MOVES OF THE PIECES

WHAT gives chess its great fascination is that the King, Queen, Rook, Bishop, Knight and Pawn move in different ways. In consequence we get a colorful diversity of possibilities unequaled in any other board game.

Before the moves and powers of the pieces are described, you should familiarize yourself with the names of three kinds of patterns of squares.

The vertical rows of squares, as we have already learned, are called *files*. They are named after the pieces which stand in them in the opening position.

The horizontal rows of squares are called *ranks*. These are *numbered* from *one* to *eight* from each side of the board.

Thus, in Diagram 2, the White Pawns are on *White's second rank*. Black's Pawns are on *Black's second rank*.

A row of squares which are all of the same color, going in the same direction, is a *diagonal*. In Diagram 2, the row of squares from White's Queen Rook (lower left corner) to Black's King Rook (upper right corner) is a *diagonal*.

Now we are ready to learn the moves of the pieces. The King's move is the simplest.

THE King can move in any direction, one square at a time.

That is to say, he can move sideways, up or down, or at an angle. *See Diagram 3.*

The King

3 *Here the King has eight possible moves. Note that the King is now on the Queen file and on the fourth rank. This square is called Q4. Why?*

4 *The King has moved along the fourth rank (sideways or horizontally) and is now on the King file. This square is called K4. Compare with Diagram 3.*

5 *Starting from Diagram 3, the King has moved along the Queen file and is now on the fifth rank. This square is called Q5. Compare with Diagram 3.*

6 *Starting from Diagram 3, the King has moved at an angle (a diagonal move) to K3. The King is now on the King file and on the third rank.*

7 The King cannot displace any of his own men, nor can he leap over them. Consequently, the King cannot make a single move in this position!

8 Still noting that the King cannot displace his own men or leap over them, we find that the King can move to Q5, Q4, Q3 and K3.

9 The King captures in the same way that he moves. That is to say, he can capture an enemy piece placed on an adjoining square. Any of the Black pieces here are liable to capture by the King.

10 The King has captured the Pawn on the King Bishop file (the King Bishop Pawn). This move is called KxBP. The King could also have captured the other Pawn (Kx QP) or the Knight (KxN).

THE Queen, like the King, can move on files, ranks and diagonals—that is to say, vertically, horizontally and at an angle.

But whereas the King can move only one square at a time, *the Queen can move the whole length of one of the lines available to her,* subject to impediments such as friendly pieces which block her path, and hostile pieces which can be captured by her.

11 *The Queen can move to any of the squares marked with an arrow. She can move along any one of the lines indicated by a series of arrows. Of course, on any one move the Queen can move in only one direction, depending on the player's choice and the nature of the position. More about this later; but turn now to Diagram 12, where all the different squares which can be reached by the Queen are listed by name. Review Diagram 3*

12 *The same diagram, but without the arrows. The Queen can move "East" on the fifth rank to K5, KB5, KN5 or KR5; or "West" on the fifth rank to QB5, QN5, QR5; or "North" on the Queen file to Q6, Q7, Q8; or "South" on the Queen file to Q4, Q3, Q2, Q1. Possible diagonal moves are to QB6, QN7, QR8 ("Northwest"); or to K6, KB7, KN8 ("Northeast"); or to K4, KB3, KN2, KR1 ("Southeast"); or to QB4, QN3, QR2 ("Southwest").*

The Queen

The Queen has the greatest powers of any piece on the chessboard!

In Diagrams 11 and 12, the Queen has a choice of no less than 27 possible moves! Powerful as the Queen is, her freedom is hampered, as we have seen, by the presence of friendly or enemy pieces.

Thus in Diagram 13 we have a dramatic object-lesson in how the Queen's mobility can be reduced by a careless player. In effect, Black is playing without the Queen. The moral of Diagram 13 is one which can be applied to good effect in the opening position (*see Diagram 14*); for we realize how important it is to create open lines for the Queen.

13 *While the White Queen has ample mobility, Black's Queen is reduced to a pitiably restricted range.*

14 *In the opening position the Queens have no move at all, as they cannot displace or leap over friendly pieces.*

As for the Queen's capturing powers (*Diagrams 15-18*), their far-ranging sweep is the scourge of the unwary!

15 *The Queen can capture the Rook by moving along the fifth rank.*

16 *Here White can play QxP or QxR (capturing diagonal moves).*

17 *Here White's Queen (now at KB6) can capture the Bishop or the Knight by making a vertical move on the King Bishop file. One direction at a time!*

18 *White has played Qx N, making a vertical move along the King Bishop file. Thus we have seen horizontal, vertical and diagonal Queen moves.*

THE Rook can move *horizontally* (on ranks) and *vertically* (on files)—in one direction at a time.

The Rook cannot move *diagonally* and is therefore not quite so strong as the Queen.

The Rook moves in only one direction at a time. It cannot displace or leap over friendly pieces.

The Rook *captures* by displacement (occupying the square of the captured piece). Its capturing moves follow the general pattern of its moves: *vertical* or *horizontal*.

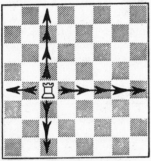

21 *The Rook can move to any of the squares marked by an arrow. Compare this Diagram with Diagram 11. You will note that the Rook cannot make the diagonal moves which are available to the Queen. The Rook has 14 possible moves; the Queen had 27!*

22 *The Rook can move (horizontally) "East" along the fourth rank to Q4, K4, KB4, KN4, KR4; or "West" along the same rank to QN4, QR4. In the Queen Bishop file the Rook can move (vertically) "North" to QB5, QB6, QB7, QB8 or "South" to QB3, QB2, QB1.*

The Rook

23 *Starting from QB4 (Diagram 21) the Rook has played from QB4 to QB8 (vertical move along the Queen Bishop file).*

24 *Starting from QB4 (Diagram 21) the Rook has played from QB4 to KN4 (horizontal move along the fourth rank).*

25 *The Rook, placed at KR5, can move along the rank and capture the Pawn.*

26 *Starting from Diagram 25, White has played RxP (horizontal move).*

27 *The Rook can capture the Bishop, but not the Knight.* The Pawn blocks its Rook's progress.

28 *White cannot play Rx N. But RxP (horizontal move) or RxB (vertical move) is feasible.*

In Diagrams 29 and 30 we see the difference in capturing powers of the Queen and Rook.

29 *The Queen can now play QxB (horizontal move) or QxN (vertical move) or QxP (diagonal move).*

30 *The Rook can now play RxB (horizontal move) or RxN (vertical move) but not RxP (diagonal move).*

LIKE the Queen, the Bishop can move and capture *diagonally*.

Unlike the Queen and Rook, the Bishop cannot move on ranks and files.

On any one move, the Bishop is limited in the following ways (we have already seen these limitations operating on King, Queen and Rook):

The move can be *in only one direction*.

The Bishop cannot leap over friendly or hostile pieces. He can capture hostile pieces by *displacement*. His own pieces act as complete stumbling blocks.

31 *The Bishop can move to any one of the thirteen squares marked with an arrow. Note that one Bishop always travels on* white *squares, while his colleague always travels on* black *squares. Thus, each Bishop controls only 32 squares.*

32 *The Bishop on Q4 can move "Northeast" to K5, KB6, KN7, KR8; "Southeast" to K3, KB2, KN1; "Southwest" to QB3, QN2, QR1; "Northwest" to QB5, QN6, QR7. All these are of course black squares.*

The Bishop

33 *The Bishop on K4 travels on* white squares, *to wit: KB5, KN6, KR7; KB3, KN2, KR1; Q3, QB2, QN1; Q5, QB6, QN7, QR8. Can you point out all these squares? Hint: these are all white squares.*

34 *Here the Bishop's mobility is greatly hampered by his own Pawns. The Bishop can move only to KB5, KN6, KR7, or Q3, QB2, QN1. "Southeast" and "Northwest" moves are impossible.*

35 *The Bishop can move "Northeast" and capture the King Rook Pawn; or move "Northwest" and capture the Queen Knight Pawn.*

36 *Again the Bishop is at K4. He can still move "Northeast" and capture the King Rook Pawn; but he cannot capture the Queen Knight Pawn. Why?*

37 *If it is White's move, he can play BxQ. If it is Black's move, he can play . . . QxB.*

38 *If it is White's move, he can play BxR. If it is Black's move, he cannot play . . . RxB.*

We place three dots in front of any Black move so that it will not be confused with a White move.

For purposes of review, return to Diagram 2. In the opening position, the Bishops are placed on the first rank. The Bishop next to the King is on KB1. The Bishop next to the Queen is on QB1.

The Bishop near the King is always called the *King Bishop*. The Bishop near the Queen is always called the *Queen Bishop*.

We have observed, in our discussion of Diagram 31, that each Bishop covers only 32 squares. In other words, each Bishop gets around quite a bit, but he can't be everywhere. Insofar as this is a weakness of the Bishop, it points up the great strength which is exerted by both Bishops. Together, your Bishops cover all 64 squares of the chessboard. For this reason, experienced players try hard to preserve the two Bishops, or Bishop-pair, against capture or exchange. There are players who will go to the greatest trouble to preserve these favorite pieces in the course of a game!

THE Knight can be described as the clown, the practical joker, the Peck's bad boy or the secret weapon of the chessboard. The Knight seems to delight in doing things differently, and in flouting the rules which are good enough for the other, orthodox, law-abiding chessmen.

For example, none of the other chessmen can leap over other pieces. The Knight *can, and does, leap over all the other forces, be they friendly or hostile.*

The other pieces have powers which are based on the dimensions of the chessboard (vertical, horizontal or diagonal moves). The Knight's move is unrelated to any of these moves.

The Queen, Rook and Bishop have moves of indeterminate length, depending on the number of squares available to them. Thus, if a Bishop is on a diagonal having seven empty squares, he can be moved one, two, three, four, five, six or seven squares, depending on the player's whim or plan. The Knight, on the other hand, has a move *which is always of the same length.*

"The old one-two" is the phrase that aptly describes the Knight's move. Each Knight move is a combination of one square and two squares:

(a) one square "North" or "South"; then two squares "East" or "West."

(b) one square "East" or "West"; then two squares "North" or "South."

The Knight

39 The Knight (now placed at Q4) can move to K6, QB6, QN5, QN3, QB2, K2, KB3, KB5. Can you see any "rhyme or reason" in these possible moves? Hint: note that the Knight's move is "L-shaped."

40 The Knight, which was at Q4, has moved to K6. He has played one square "East" and two squares "North." This combination of one square and two squares forms a capital "L."

41 Starting from Diagram 39, the Knight has moved from Q4 to KB3: one square "South" and two squares "East."

42 Starting from Diagram 39, the Knight has moved from Q4 to QB6: one square "West" and two squares "North."

43 The Knight, now on K5, cannot capture either Black Pawn.

44 The Knight, however, can leap disdainfully over the Black Pawns to reach QB6.

45 Here the Knight leaps over friendly men to reach QB6.

46 See the previous diagram. The Knight leaps over friend and enemy.

47 The Knight, now on Q3, can capture the Bishop.

48 White has played Nx B; the Knight is on QB5.

49 The Knight (now on QB4) can capture only one Pawn—which one?

50 The Knight has captured the King Pawn—the only possible capture.

Studying Diagrams 43-50, we see that the Knight can leap over friendly or hostile men; but as for capturing, he can take pieces only on the *terminal* square of his move. If we think of the Knight as moving three squares, *he can capture only on the final square.*

51 *Here the Knight can leap over any of the Black men, but he cannot capture any of them.*

52 *If it is White's move, he can capture the hostile Knight. If it is Black's turn, he can play . . . NxN.*

53 *As for the other pieces, they capture the Knight in their usual manner.*

54 *The Queen, which was on K3, has played QxN. (QxR was also possible.)*

A final point about the Knight: at the beginning of the game (*see Diagram 2*) the King Knight is placed at KN1 between the King Rook and the King Bishop. The Queen Knight is placed on QN1 between the Queen Rook and the Queen Bishop.

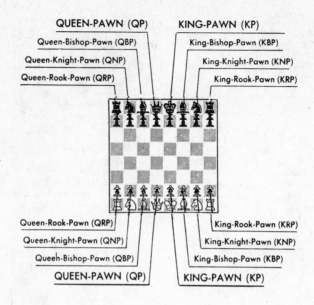

QUEEN-PAWN (QP)   KING-PAWN (KP)

Queen-Bishop-Pawn (QBP)   King-Bishop-Pawn (KBP)

Queen-Knight-Pawn (QNP)   King-Knight-Pawn (KNP)

Queen-Rook-Pawn (QRP)   King-Rook-Pawn (KRP)

Queen-Rook-Pawn (QRP)   King-Rook-Pawn (KRP)

Queen-Knight-Pawn (QNP)   King-Knight-Pawn (KNP)

Queeh-Bishop-Pawn (QBP)   King-Bishop-Pawn (KBP)

QUEEN-PAWN (QP)   KING-PAWN (KP)

The Pawn

THE Pawn has a number of interesting differences from the other chessmen.

The Pawn, for example, can move in only one direction: *forward*.

The Pawn is the only one of the chessmen which captures in a manner different from the way in which it moves.

There are several other peculiarities in the Pawn's powers which we shall encounter later on.

Refreshing your memory by studying the diagram on page 24, you will recall that in *the opening position* all White Pawns are on White's second rank; all Black Pawns are on Black's second rank.

White Pawns *always* move "North." Black Pawns *always* move "South."

55 *The Pawn advances one square at a time.*

56 *The Pawn at K4 has moved to K5.*

57 *Black Pawns move "South." The Pawn at Black's K4 advances.*

58 *Black's Pawn, moving "South," has played . . . P-K5.*

The first time any Pawn moves, at any stage of the game, it has the option of advancing *one* or *two* squares. On any *subsequent* moves of that Pawn, it can only move one square.

59 *White wants to move his Queen Pawn. He decides to move it* <u>one</u> *square.*

60 *Starting from Diagram 59, White has advanced the Queen Pawn one square (P–Q3).*

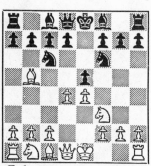

61 *Had White decided, in the position of Diagram 59, to advance his Queen Pawn two squares (P–Q4), the above would be the result.*

62 *White has decided to move the Queen Pawn again.* <u>Now it can move only one square.</u> *Above is the position resulting from the advance (P–Q5).*

63 To review: White's Pawn is on the third rank; hence it has made its first move. It can now advance only one square.

64 Starting from Diagram 63, White's King Bishop Pawn has moved "North." This would be written: P–KB4.

65 More review: Black's Pawn is on the fourth rank.* It can only advance one square.

66 Starting from Diagram 65, Black has moved "South." This move is ...P–QB5.*

---

* Remember that Black's ranks (and moves) are counted from *his* side of the board. Thus, White's *fourth* rank is Black's *fifth* rank. More about this on pages 38-39. *See also* Diagrams 57-58.

We come now to the Pawn's capturing powers. We have seen that the Pawn moves vertically along the files. But in capturing, the Pawn takes the piece or Pawn which is *diagonally forward on adjoining squares*, not the piece on the square directly ahead of it.

67 *The Pawn cannot move, nor can it capture the Bishop.*

68 *Neither Pawn can advance or capture. The Pawns block each other.*

69 *If White moves, he plays PxB.*

70 *This is the position resulting from PxB.*

To put it another way: the Pawn *moves* like a miniature Rook; it *captures* like a miniature Bishop!

Still another way: White Pawns move "North." They capture "Northwest" or "Northeast." Black Pawns move "South." They capture "Southeast" or "Southwest."

The photograph illustrates the Pawn's capturing powers. White, to move, has the choice of PxN or PxR.

The White Pawn can capture the Rook or Knight

HOW TO WIN

MEMORIZE: you win a game of chess by attacking the hostile King in such a way that no matter what your opponent does, his King cannot escape capture.

When either King is attacked, he is said to be *in check*.

When the attack is of the kind against which there is no defense, the King is said to be *checkmated:* the game is over.

71 *White's Queen attacks the Black King; how does the King get out of check?*

72 *The Black Pawn has captured the Queen; Black's King is no longer in check.*

73 *Here Black has moved his King, getting out of check.*

74 *Here Black has "interposed" his Rook. His King is out of check.*

Thus we see that there are three ways to answer a check:

Capture the checking piece (Diagram 72).

Move the King out of attacking range (Diagram 73).

Interpose between the King and the checking piece (Diagram 74).

But suppose none of these three methods are available? In that case, the King is checkmated.

Checkmate

BEFORE we go on, we must learn two important facts which have a bearing on checkmate positions:

(1) The King is never actually captured. Merely trapping the King without leaving him any chance of escape ends the game at once.

(2) The King must never play to a square which is within the capturing range of enemy forces.

75 *Black's King is in check (horizontal attack by White's Rook). Black cannot play...K–R1 or...K–B1 because that would leave him in check.*

76 *Black has played... K–R2 and is now out of check. ...K–N2 or ... K–B2 would of course have served the purpose just as well. Compare Diagram 77.*

77 *Black's King has only one move to get out of check. Can you find that move?*

78 *...K–R2 was the only move (...K–R1 or...K–B1 would still leave the King in check).*

79 *Again the Black King is in check, but this time he has no escape. (In the event of ...K-R1 or ... K-B1 the King would still be in check.)* This is checkmate! *This pattern is frequently encountered.*

80 *Another example of checkmate. ...K-R1 or ...K-B1 will not do; while...K-R2 or...K-N2 or ...K-B2 is ruled out by the presence of White's King,* which commands those squares.*

Basically, games are decided by checkmate. However, a player may surrender (*resign* is the technical term) long before checkmate arrives. Why is this?

As we have seen from Diagrams 80 and 81, King and Queen or King and Rook can enforce checkmate. Consequently, if you are a Rook or Queen ahead, your opponent may prefer to resign rather than play out glumly to checkmate.

Generally a player who has gained material in this way will try to exchange as many forces as possible (i.e engage in reciprocal captures) until a simpli-

---

* Always bear in mind that a King cannot expose himself to attack by hostile forces. In this case, the Black King cannot move to squares commanded by the White King.

fied position is reached where checkmate can be forced.

In many a game, however, it becomes possible to attack the hostile King at a fairly early stage by means of a highly concentrated assault.

81 *This is also checkmate. The Queen, possessing the horizontal moving powers of the Rook, can give checkmate in the same way. We come now to an important idea: The King cannot capture a hostile piece if he thereby exposes himself to capture by another enemy piece.*

82 *Here is the method of checkmate just alluded to. ...K–R1 or ...K–B1 cannot be played, as the Queen attacks those squares. ...KxQ is impossible, because that would subject Black's King to the attack of White's King. ...K–B2 and ...K–R2 are also unplayable. Why?*

At this stage, these are the two important points to bear in mind:

(1) You win by checkmating your opponent's King. (See pages 77-82 for examples of the elementary checkmates.)

(2) You win by achieving so great a superiority of force that your opponent resigns.

VALUES OF THE CHESSMEN

YOU have seen that the Queen is much the strongest piece on the chessboard. The Rook is next in power; then comes the Bishop.

How shall we assess the Knight? His move is a short one, not to be compared in range with that of the Bishop; yet a Bishop can cover only 32 squares of the chessboard, while the Knight, who plays to a square of opposite color on each move, can sooner or later reach every square on the board.*

Experience has shown that the Bishop and Knight are of approximately equal value.

The Pawn is the weakest of the chessmen, as we might expect from its short-range moves. (Later on, however, we shall find that the Pawn has remarkable powers!)

We cannot measure the King's value, which is infinite.

---

* If the Knight is on a white square, his next move will land him on a black square. If the Knight is on a black square, his next move will land him on a white square. Try this out: put a White Knight at KN1 (black square). Play him to KB3 (white square) and then to K5 (black square) etc.

The following table of values is accepted as standard:

Queen	♛	9 points
Rook	♜	5 points
Bishop	♝	3 points
Knight	♞	3 points
Pawn	♟	1 point

In actual practice, most games are decided by superiority of force. For this reason, it is essential to maintain equality of material.

The value of this table is at once apparent. It shows, for example, that you can readily give up a Knight to get a Bishop in return (or vice versa). To give up the Queen for a Pawn would, however, be idiotic, unless a very important return (such as checkmate) were immediately available.

Similarly, to give up a Rook for a Bishop would not be good, unless one picked up several Pawns to make the transaction a fairly even one.

CHESS NOTATION

BLACK

QR8	QN8	QB8	Q8	K8	KB8	KN8	KR8
QR7	QN7	QB7	Q7	K7	KB7	KN7	KR7
QR6	QN6	QB6	Q6	K6	KB6	KN6	KR6
QR5	QN5	QB5	Q5	K5	KB5	KN5	KR5
QR4	QN4	QB4	Q4	K4	KB4	KN4	KR4
QR3	QN3	QB3	Q3	K3	KB3	KN3	KR3
QR2	QN2	QB2	Q2	K2	KB2	KN2	KR2
QR1	QN1	QB1	Q1	K1	KB1	KN1	KR1

WHITE

B EFORE we go on to playing over games, we want to familiarize ourselves thoroughly with the chess notation—the art of recording chess moves.

We have already learned quite a bit about the notation in an informal way. We know, for example, how the pieces are named from the positions they have at the beginning of the game. For review purposes, see the chart above, in which the names of all the squares are set forth clearly.

The names of the Pawns, systematically presented in the chart on page 24, likewise offer no difficulty. (Remember, however, that a Pawn changes its name every time it captures!)

For a quick review of files and ranks, take the following two diagrams:

83 *The Queen file.*

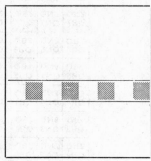

84 *A Rank.*

As for ranks, we know that each player numbers them from his side of the board:

| 8 WHITE'S EIGHTH RANK |
| 7 |
| 6 |
| 5 |
| 4 |
| 3 |
| 2 |
| 1 WHITE'S FIRST RANK |

85 *The ranks numbered from White's side of the board.*

| 1 BLACK'S FIRST RANK |
| 2 |
| 3 |
| 4 |
| 5 |
| 6 |
| 7 |
| 8 BLACK'S 8TH RANK |

86 *The ranks numbered from Black's side of the board.*

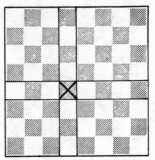

87 *The eight files (same names for White and Black pieces).*

88 *The marked square is Q4 for a White move, or Q5 for a Black move.*

We are now ready for some "Chess Movies" (games presented in diagram style) which will enable you to become more expert in reading chess notation and which will give you impressive examples of checkmate.*

Game 1: Bishop's Opening

91 *White plays 1 P–K4.*

92 *Black plays 1...P–K4.*

---

* Each diagram shows the position existing *before* the moves which appear below that diagram.

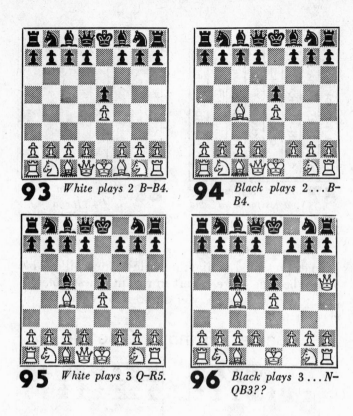

93 *White plays 2 B–B4.*

94 *Black plays 2 . . . B–B4.*

95 *White plays 3 Q–R5.*

96 *Black plays 3 . . . N–QB3??*

Note that Black's third move is followed by question marks, the customary device to indicate a bad move. Good moves are indicated by exclamation marks.

By playing 3 . . . N-QB3?? Black was guarding his King Pawn from attack. He failed to realize, however, that White was also menacing the King Bishop Pawn as well.

97 *White plays 4 QxBP mate.* **98** *Black is checkmated!*

The position in Diagram 98 is checkmate because Black's King cannot escape; Black cannot interpose against the check; nor can he capture the White Queen, which is defended by the White Bishop. (*See Diagram 82.*)

If the score of this game is recorded in the orthodox manner, we get:

White			Black
1	P-K4	P-K4	
2	B-B4	B-B4	
3	Q-R5	N-QB3??	
4	QxBP mate		

(Mate is the usual shortened term for checkmate.)

Check all moves against the diagrams to make sure that you understand the powers of the pieces and the method of recording their moves.

Now let us try a second "Chess Movie," giving the game a bit more detailed attention.

Game 2: Petroff Defense

99 1 P-K4   P-K4
Both players do well to begin by moving a center Pawn, which enables them to get their pieces out rapidly.

100 2 N-KB3 N-KB3
White brings out his King Knight attacking Black's King Pawn. Black does the same, attacking White's King Pawn.

101 3 NxP   N-B3
White captures the King Pawn and Black brings out ("develops") his Queen Knight. White will now be a Pawn ahead.

102 4 NxN   QPxN
White captures the Knight and Black recaptures with his Queen Pawn, opening up a line for his Queen Bishop.

Here the play is more complex than in the previous game. Black wins by an amazing Queen "sacrifice" which completely baffles his opponent. "Sacrificing" is an important device which is explained during the course of the game.

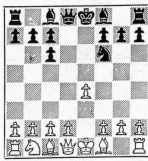

103 5 P-Q3   B-QB4
White protects his King Pawn* and Black develops still another piece. Note this: Black has two pieces out, White has none. Black is ready for action.

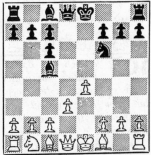

104 6 B-N5   NxP!!
White plays out his Queen Bishop and Black "sacrifices"** his Queen. White can now win the Queen, obtaining a great advantage in material.

---

* We say that the King Pawn is protected because if Black plays . . . NxP then White can reply PxN. Thus White would win a Knight in return for a Pawn. From the table of relative values (p. 36) we know that this transaction is good for White, bad for Black.

** Greater material is often lost in return for lesser material through oversights. When the loss is *intentional*, it is termed a "sacrifice." The player who sacrifices, hopes, of course, to gain back more than he has lost.

105 *7 BxQ   BxPch*
White naturally
snaps at the valuable Queen,
but now Black reveals the
purpose of the "sacrifice":
first comes a check to which
there is only one reply.

106 *8 KxB or 8 K-*
Q2 is now impossi-
ble. (White cannot subject
his King to attack by the
Black Knight.) So White
plays:

        8 K-K2   . . . .

107 *8 . . . .   B-N5ch*
Another check . . .
White cannot interpose to the
Bishop check. He cannot cap-
ture either Bishop or the
Knight.

108 Nor can White
move his King: K-
K1 or K-B3 or K-K3 or K-
Q2—impossible moves every
one of them! White is checkmated.

MORE ABOUT THE KING

IN view of the King's all-important character, you will not be surprised that there are more things to be learned about this vital piece. These details are easy to grasp and fit usefully into the pattern of an ordinary game.

First we encounter some methods of attack which may be extremely dangerous; then, by way of compensation, we discover a most effective way of ensuring the King's safety.

Discovered Check

109 *First, by way of review, we give an orthodox check. See Diagram 110.*

110 *The Queen has moved from K2 to K5 to give a diagonal check.*

This type of check, where a piece moves to a square from which it can give check, is quite familiar by now.

But there are other positions, in which a piece *which is not giving check, can attack the King without moving!*

111 *The White Queen on K5 is not giving check, as its action is blocked by the White Pawn on KB6. But suppose that Pawn advances?*

112 *White has played P–B7ch—a discovered check. By advancing, the Pawn opens up the line of attack against Black's King.*

Now, if you are of an inventive turn of mind, you can envisage some of the nasty possibilities inherent in a discovered check: suppose that as the line of attack is "discovered" for a check, the piece which is opening the line *attacks another piece at the same time?*

113 White plays R–Q7ch. His Bishop attacks the Black King; his Rook attacks the Black Queen!

114 Black MUST move his King or interpose his Queen, to get out of check. Either way, his Queen is lost!

Sometimes there is a defense to such dastardly discovered checks. If the piece which is secondarily attacked, can run away to *interpose* against the check, all is well:

115 White plays P–B6 ch expecting to win the Queen. But this time Black can escape by interposing!

116 Black has avoided disaster by playing ...Q–N3. The King is out of check, the Queen is safe. A narrow escape.

Double Check

THIS is an even more venomous form of discovered check. Here the piece which moves away to open a line, *also* gives check. Hence the term *double* check.

117 *Here White plays B–B6ch, giving check with the Queen and Bishop.*

118 *Black must move his King; he cannot capture Queen or Bishop.*

Note these points about double check. If either checking piece is *en prise*,* or even both, neither can be captured, for then the other piece would still be giving check. Hence, in Diagram 118, neither... QxQ nor...PxB is possible. By the same line of reasoning, interposition is impossible, for there is no way of interposing against *both* checks. So, in reply to a double check, a King move is the only way out.

---

* When a piece is under attack, it is said to be *en prise* (on preez).

Suppose a King move is impossible? Then we get a situation like the following:

119 *White gives a dou-ble check with B–B6ch.*

120 *Checkmate! The King has no es-cape.*

Very often a double check can be quite profitable. Here is an example:

121 *QxQch would get White nowhere, as Black simply replies...PxQ. But B–B6ch wins the Black Queen.*

122 *Black MUST play ...K–N1, where-upon White plays BxQ. Black was helpless against the double check.*

Forking Checks

ONE of the most dreaded powers of the Knight is his ability to "fork" two pieces—that is, attack them simultaneously. When one of the attacked pieces is the King, the Knight often does considerable damage.

Diagrams 123 and 124 illustrate a forking check. This is the most effective kind of fork, if you are administering it; and the worst kind of fork, if you are on the receiving end. The power of this type of fork lies in the attack on the King: the King must get out of check, and the other piece under attack *has to be left to its fate*. In Diagram 123 the "other piece" happens to be the Queen, and to lose this valuable piece under such circumstances is equivalent to losing the game.

123 *The Knight has a deadly fork by going to K5 with check. The King will have to move, and the Queen will be lost, with ruinous loss of material by White.*

124 *Black would like to save his Queen, but he has no choice: he MUST move his King, allowing White to play NxQ. A very profitable transaction for White.*

Castling

Now that we have learned so many new ways of badgering the King, it will be soothing to acquaint ourselves with an excellent method of making the King's life healthier and longer.

This method is known as castling, and it has many curious features. The most important one is that it is the only move in the game in which you are allowed to move two pieces. *This double move counts for only one move!* Now let us see how this unique move is made.

The two pieces which execute castling are the *King* (of course) and either *Rook.** Castling with the King Rook (on the King-side) is known as *King-side castling.* Castling with the Queen Rook (on the Queen-side) is known as *Queen-side castling.*

125 *White is about to castle King-side.*

126 *White has castled on the King-side.*

---

* In the old days, the piece we now call a Rook was generally called a "Castle." This term still prevails in whodunits and in historical novels.

The mechanism is simple enough:

(a) move the King next to the Rook.

(b) move the King Rook from the King's right to the King's left.

(This move is written O-O.)

For Black the procedure is the same:

127 *Black to play O–O.*

128 *Black has played O-O.*

Now let us see how the process works on a crowded chessboard:

129 *White to play O–O.*

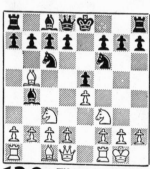

130 *White has played O-O.*

131 *Black to play 0-0.*

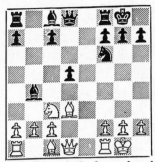

132 *Black has played ...0-0.*

The inexperienced player does well to castle early on the King-side almost as a matter of course. In this way he will quickly shield his King from heavy attack and will also bring his King Rook into the game.

133 *White to castle Queen-side (0-0-0).*

134 *White has castled Queen-side (0-0-0).*

135 *Black to play . . . O-O-O.*

136 *Black has played . . . O-O-O.*

Castling Queen-side is a trifle more complex, for here there are *three* squares between the King and Queen Rook. The King moves to QB1, the Queen Rook goes to Q1, thus:

137 *White to play O-O-O.*

138 *White has played O-O-O.*

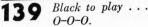

139 *Black to play . . . 0-0-0.*

140 *Black has played . . . 0-0-0.*

Now for the special rules about castling. You cannot castle when:

(a) Your King is in check.

(b) Your King has moved previously.

(c) The Rook which you wish to use for castling has moved previously.

(d) A hostile piece commands the square (KN1 or QB1) to which the King is to move in castling.

(e) A hostile piece commands the square (KB1 or Q1) over which the King has to pass in castling.

(f) A hostile piece stands between the King and the castling Rook.

(g) A friendly piece stands between the King and the castling Rook.

These exceptions are pictured in Diagrams 141-148, on the next two pages.

141 *White's King is in check; hence he cannot castle at this point. Later on it may be possible to castle, if none of the exceptions apply. See Rule (a).*

142 *Here Black's King has already moved; hence he will never be able to castle at any time in this game. See Rule (b) to verify this point.*

143 *White can never castle Queen-side, but King-side castling is still feasible, and can be played in this situation. See Rule (c).*

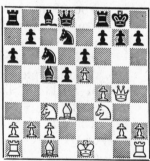

144 *Castling King-side is temporarily impossible for White, as his KN1 is controlled by Black's Queen Bishop. See Rule (d).*

The four cases shown above in which castling is impossible, are the ones seen most frequently in practical play. Nevertheless, every player should be familiar with the remaining exceptions.

145 *Here Black cannot castle because his KB1 is commanded by White's Queen Bishop. See Rule (e).*

146 *Here Black cannot castle because of the presence of White's Bishop. See Rule (f).*

147 *White cannot castle on either wing because of the White pieces which act as obstacles. See rule (g).*

148 *Black can play . . . 0–0–0 despite the fact that his Rook will pass over a square (QN1) commanded by the White Queen.*

THE VALUE OF CASTLING

149 *The opening moves:*
1 P–K4   P–K4
2 N–KB3   N–QB3
3 B–N5   . . . .

This is the Ruy Lopez, one of the favorite opening lines in modern chess.

150 *The game continues:*
3 . . . .   N–B3
4 O–O   . . . .

White castles early, hoping that his King Rook will see useful action. His expectations are fulfilled.

151 4 . . . .   NxP
5 R–K1   . . . .

Black captures the King Pawn, and the King Rook wheels into action, threatening 6 RxN. Hence Black retreats the Knight.

152 5 . . . .   N–Q3
6 N–B3   NxB

You would now expect 7 NxN in reply, but White scents the possibility of action against Black's uncastled King!

153 7 NxP! NxN (B6)
*Black is two pieces
ahead. But his joy is short-
lived: the following discovered check is crushing, as King
and Queen are menaced.*

154 8 NxN dis ch . . . .
*A terrible situation
for Black. His King is attacked by the check from White's
Rook, his Queen is attacked
by White's Knight.*

155 8 . . . . B–K2
*Maybe it isn't so
bad after all, Black says to
himself; White's Queen is
also en prise to Black's
Knight!*

156 9 NxB!! . . . .
*This surprising
move does not leave Black
much choice (if 9 . . . QxN;
10 RxQch, KxR; 11 QPxN
with crushing advantage).*

157 9 . . . . NxQ
He has nothing better, but now comes another nasty discovered check *which assures White a lasting material advantage.*

158 10 N-N6 dis ch. . . .
This forces Black's reply, both . . . K-B1 and . . . K-K2 being obviously impossible. (Remember, the King cannot walk into attack!)

159 10 . . . Q-K2; 11 NxQ. *B l a c k 's knight on Q8 is stranded and cannot escape. Black will therefore come out a clear piece down. In addition, White t h r e a t e n s N-N6, with a terrific discovered check, winning Black's KR.*

160 *If Black tries to avoid the discovered check with 11 . . . K-B1, there follows 12 NxB . . . RxN; 13 RxN, and Black has lost a clear piece. This material disadvantage should lose the game for him.*

DRAWN GAMES

U P to this point you have been left with the impression that all games have a decisive result, either by enforced checkmate or by resignation. It is true that the majority of games of chess wind up in a decisive manner. But another kind of result is possible: *the draw*. A drawn game is one in which there is no decision: no victory, no defeat.

Now there are various ways in which a drawn result may be arrived at. The most frequent one is by agreement of both players. The position may lack interest, the hour may be late, a cautious player may be too timid to continue, a reckless player may have overreached himself. Whatever the cause, a draw can always be declared when both players agree to it.

Then there are two provisions in the official laws of chess which make a draw possible.

One of these provisions is the "50-move" rule, which states that if, within the past 50 moves, no capture has been made and no Pawn moved, either side may claim a draw. The object of this rule is to penalize players who are incapable of realizing an advantage, and to protect players from opponents who refuse to agree to a draw when there is no real basis for winning.

The other rule is that when a position is repeated three times, *a draw may be claimed by the player who is about to make the move which will bring about the threefold repetition.*

In actual play among average players, the 50-move rule and the repetition rule play a very small role. More important are the three drawing methods known as *perpetual check, stalemate,* and *insufficient mating material.*

Perpetual Check

THIS is a self-explanatory term, applicable to positions in which a player makes it obvious that he can check his opponent's King indefinitely—"perpetually." Perpetual check is a particularly useful device in situations where a player would be hopelessly lost without this resource.

161 *White is a Rook down, and ordinarily his game would be quite hopeless. But there follows:*

  1 Q–K8ch   K–R2
  2 Q–R5ch   . . . .

162 *Can the checks be stopped?*

  2 . . . .   K–N1
  3 Q–K8ch   K–R2
  4 Q–R5ch   . . . .

And Black must agree to a draw, as his King can never escape the checks!

It follows that perpetual check is a drawing device which should be watched for early when you have a bad game, for this may be the only way to ward off disaster. Conversely, when you have the advantage, you must be on the alert lest a perpetual check by your opponent rob you of the fruits of victory. Positions where a King is exposed to attack are particularly conducive to perpetual check. Incidentally, most perpetual checks are given by the Queen—natural enough, because of the enormous cruising range at the disposal of this powerful piece.

Stalemate

THE difference between checkmate (which wins) and stalemate (which only draws), is slight. But slight as that difference is, it is vital.

Your King *is in check;* it is your turn to move; you have no legal move;* you are *checkmated.*

But, *if your King is not in check;* it is your turn to move; and you have no legal move available, then you are *stalemated,* and the game is drawn.

Checkmate and stalemate are alike in that they both apply to a player who is on the move, and who has no legal move left. Checkmate and stalemate differ in this: *if the King is already in check,* then checkmate results; *if the King is not in check,* then stalemate results.

---

* The laws of chess do not permit the King to move to a square controlled by enemy forces. In answer to a check, the laws of chess permit only moves that, in one way or another, do away with the check.

163 *Black's King is in check, but he has any number of legal moves: ...K–R2 or ...K–N2 or ... K–B2. Obviously this is neither checkmate nor stalemate.*

164 *Black's King is not in check, but he has an ample number of legal moves, ...K–N1 or ...K–R2 or ...K–N2. This is neither checkmate nor stalemate.*

165 *Black's King is in check, and ...K– R2 or ... K–N2 or ...K– N1 is impossible, all these squares being covered by White pieces.* This is checkmate.

166 *Black's King is not in check, but he has no legal moves, ... K– N1 or ...K–N2 or ...K–R2 being impossible.* This is a case of stalemate.

167 *Again it is Black's move. Is he stalemated? No! For he can play ...P-B5—a perfectly legal move.*

168 *Again it is Black's move. Is he stalemated? Yes! His Pawn is blocked, and his King has no legal move.*

169 *White to move, is stalemated!*

170 *White to move, is stalemated!*

Mating Material

THE minimum forces needed to checkmate a lone King are:

    (a) King and Queen.
    (b) King and Rook.
    (c) King and two Bishops.
    (d) King and Bishop and Knight.

There are also times when King and Pawn can win against a lone King (see page 68).

Checkmate by force is impossible if you have only a Bishop, or a Knight, or even two Knights, left against a lone King. The following is a drawn position:

171 *With only a Knight ahead, White can never win the game. This is a clear draw.*

172 *With only a Bishop ahead, White can never win the game. This is a clear draw.*

It is only at the very end of the game that the advantage of a Bishop or a Knight ahead will not win. King and Bishop vs. King or King and Knight vs. King is a draw; but in the earlier stages of the game, when there is plenty of material on the board, the advantage of the piece ahead will be decisive in 99% of all the possible cases you may encounter. The extra piece almost always allows you to win easily in one of two ways:

(a) The extra piece enables you to mount an attack against the King which your opponent cannot parry.

(b) The extra piece enables you to concentrate your forces to win more material.

MORE ABOUT THE PAWN

Nᴏᴛ long ago we said that there are positions in which King and Pawn can force a win against a lone King. On the face of it, this statement seems absurd: the Pawn is much weaker than the Bishop or Knight, neither of which can force checkmate. How then can the Pawn force checkmate?

Pawn Promotion

To answer this question, we must describe a power of the Pawn which has not been mentioned up to this point:

When a Pawn reaches the eighth rank, it can be promoted to a Queen or Rook or Bishop or Knight. The Pawn is simply removed from the board, to be replaced by a piece of your own choosing. As a rule, the Queen is the piece selected—in, say 99% of all instances. The Queen being the strongest piece on the board, this choice is as natural as it is logical.

The fact that you may still have your original Queen does not prevent you from acquiring a second Queen—or even a third or fourth! The fact that you may still have both Rooks does not prevent you from acquiring a third Rook. It is theoretically possible (but practically very rare indeed) to acquire a third Bishop or third Knight.

Now you see how King and Pawn often win against the King. If your Pawn can be promoted to Queen, you have the ending King and Queen vs. King, in which it is possible to force checkmate.

There is such a disparity between the powers of the Pawn and Queen that the sudden change, once a Pawn has been Queened, must strike the beginner with dramatic force. The contrast is effectively brought out in Diagrams 173-176, where a "lowly" Pawn becomes a rampaging Queen. The Black Rook, which seems so powerful, becomes a wretched victim.

173 *Ordinarily Rook wins against Pawn, but not here. White plays 1 P-K8(Q)ch. Black MUST move his King.*

174 *White advanced the Pawn to the eighth rank, removed the Pawn and replaced it with a Queen.*

175 *Black has moved his King out of check, but now he must lose the Rook.*

176 *White has played QxR and can now proceed to force checkmate.*

King and Bishop vs. King is only a draw, but with Pawns on the board, the material advantage wins easily.

177 *As...K–K5 is impossible, Black must give up the protection of his Bishop Pawn. There follows:*

1 . . . .   **K–K3**
2 KxP   . . . .

178 *Now White will win the remaining Black Pawn, and will then force the promotion of his own Pawn. The process is an easy one. It will repay careful study.*

Where the Pawn succeeds in Queening, or threatens to Queen, by means of capture, the process is apt to be painfully expensive for the other player. The gain of material is often so great, with or without Queening, that immediate victory becomes possible.

179 *This time it is Black who is doing the Queening:*

1 . . . .   P–R8(Q)
2 RxQ   PxR(Q)

180 *This was a case in which a Pawn became a Queen by making a capture on the last rank.*

181 *Immediate Queening will not do, as Black simply replies . . . RxQ. So White plays 1 R–Q8! leaving Black helpless.*

182 *White threatens 2 P–B8(Q) or 2 Rx Rch, KxR; 3 P–B8(Q)ch. Black has no defense: (if) 1 . . . RxR; 2 PxR(Q)ch etc.*

Sometimes Queening fails of its immediate purpose: the newly-Queened Pawn is at once captured. However, such gains of the Queen are apt to be costly. For example:

183 *Material is even, but White can win a Rook:*

1 P–B8(Q)   RxQ
2 RxRch   . . . .

184 *Material is no longer even. White's attempt to get a new Queen has "failed," but he is now a Rook to the good.*

Game 3: Caro-Kann Defense *

With this drastic and impressive example of the dynamic values of Pawn promotion, we conclude this section. One important facet of the Pawn's promotional powers is the realization that the Pawn cannot be treated with contempt. Every Pawn is a potential Queen. The win of a Pawn carries with it the

---

* This opening is named after two nineteenth century players, Horatio Caro and Marcus Kann, who popularized this line of play.

promise that the player who has obtained the material advantage may very likely be able to acquire another Queen.

185 The game begins:
1 P–K4   P–QB3
2 P–Q4   P–Q4
3 N–QB3   PxP

186 4 NxP   N–B3
5 N–N3   P–KR4
Now White should play 6 P–KR4 to prevent . . . P–R5.

187 6 B–KN5   P–R5!
An embarrassing move for White, as N–B5 or N–K4 is impossible, while 6 N(N3)–K2 blocks his pieces.

188 7 BxN   PxN
8 B–K5   RxP
9 RxR   . . . .
White expects 9 . . . PxR; 10 BxRP with even material.

189 9 . . . . *Q–R4 ch!*
10 *P–B3* . . . .
Black plans an amazing Queen sacrifice with a subtle point.

190 10 . . . . *QxB ch!!*
Black gives up his Queen for only a Bishop; but he will get a new Queen— and more!

191 11 *PxQ* *PxR*
White has an enormous material advantage; and what does he do but resign! What is the explanation?

192 *Black threatens 12 . . . PxN(Q) or . . . P–R8(Q). He cannot be prevented from obtaining a new Queen, remaining at least a piece ahead!*

Capturing En Passant

CAPTURING en passant (in passing) is a special power a Pawn gains, when it reaches fifth rank, which allows it to capture an opposing Pawn if the opposing Pawn should pass it by on its first move (when, ordinarily, it can be advanced two squares). The use of this power is not common in actual play, but it is sometimes threatened, and an understanding of its mechanism is essential.

Capturing en passant is an option which must be exercised as soon as the hostile Pawn advances from the second to the fourth rank. If the capture is not made *in reply*, it cannot be made at all.

The capturing Pawn must be on its fifth rank. A Pawn located on any other rank cannot capture en passant.

Capturing en passant is impossible where it would expose your own King to check; for then capturing en passant becomes an illegal move.

It is interesting to note how the en passant rule came into being. Five or six centuries ago, Pawns could move only one square on the first move, thus leading to a game full of blockaded files. Players in that era thought the game would be improved if they were given the option of moving Pawns two squares at the start so that the major pieces could be developed faster and files and diagonals opened.

Since it was obviously unfair to allow a Pawn, by use of this privilege, to escape capture from an opposing Pawn that had reached fifth rank, the en passant power was agreed upon.

193 *It is Black's move. He advances the Queen Pawn one square, leading to the position of Diagram 194.*

194 *This illustrates the normal capturing position. Black has advanced his Pawn only one square and White's Pawn can capture him.*

195 *But, let's say that Black advances his Queen Pawn two squares, as shown here. White can take advantage of the en passant power by playing PxP, resulting in the position shown in Diagram 196.*

196 *The position resulting from PxP (e.p.) is the same as would have arisen if Black had advanced his Pawn only one square.*

ELEMENTARY CHECKMATES

THE study of the elementary checkmates is useful to the beginner, partly because they illustrate the basic technique for bringing a game to a successful conclusion, partly because they give valuable insights into the power of the chess forces.

The mate with the Queen is by far the easiest, as we would expect from the enormous power of this piece. The only (occasional) difficulty is that *stalemate possibilities must be avoided!*

197

	1 K-B2	K-Q4
	2 K-Q3	K-B4
	3 Q-B6	K-Q4

White has already limited the mobility of Black's King to a considerable extent.

198

	4 Q-K7	K-B3
	5 K-B4	K-N3
	6 Q-Q7	K-R3

At last the Black King has been forced to the side of the board.

199 7 K–B5   K–R4
8 Q–R7 mate
(Another way was 8 Q–N5 mate.)

200 *This is checkmate because the Black King is in check and has no legal moves.*

The mate with the Rook is slower—just what we would expect, as the Rook is weaker than the Queen. The overall process is the same: the gradual approach of the stronger side's King, *followed by a strategic move with the Rook to cut off the lone King's command of a large segment of the board.*

As the Rook cannot attack diagonal-wise, the weaker side's King has considerable leeway of escape. But the skillful maneuvering of King and Rook forces the mate by an effective attrition process which deserves careful study.

201

1 K-N2   K-Q5
2 K-B2   K-K5
3 K-B3   K-K4
4 K-B4   K-K5
5 R-K1ch! K-B4

The Black King is cut off from five files. The process is now repeated.

202

6 K-Q4   K-B5
7 R-B1ch! K-N4
8 K-K4   K-N3
9 K-K5   K-N4
10 R-N1ch! K-R4

The Black King has been forced to the side of the board.

203

11 K-B4   K-R3
12 K-B5   K-R2
13 K-B6   K-R1
14 K-B7   K-R2
15 R-R1 mate

204

Again we have a checkmating position: Black's King is in check and has no legal move for escape purposes.

The mate with two Bishops is a bit more difficult; but the cooperation of the two Bishops is a thing of beauty.

205

1	B–K1	K–Q6
2	K–N2	K–K7
3	B–KB2	K–Q6
4	K–B3	K–B6
5	K–K4	K–B5
6	B–Q4	K–N5

The Black King is to be driven to his QR1.

206

7	B–Q1	K–B5
8	B–QB2	K–N5
9	K–Q5	K–N4
10	B–QB5	K–R3
11	K–B6	K–R4
12	B–Q6	K–R3

The Black King is being forced back.

207

13	B–N4	K–R2
14	K–B7	K–R3
15	B–Q3ch	K–R2
16	B–B5ch	K–R1
17	B–K4 mate	

The mate with the two Bishops can only be given in a corner.

208 *This is clearly a checkmate position. Black's King is in check, and has no legal move to escape checkmate. Between them the Bishops cover all the 64 squares of the board, making checkmate possible.*

The mate with Bishop and Knight is quite difficult, but it has the charm of being rigorously systematic.

209

1	N-N3ch	K-B3
2	K-N4	K-Q4
3	B-B3ch	K-Q3
4	N-Q4	K-K4
5	K-B4	K-B3
6	K-Q5	K-B2
7	N-B5	K-B3
8	N-Q6	K-N3
9	K-K5	K-N2
10	B-K4	K-N1

210

11	K-B6	K-R1
12	N-B7ch	K-N1
13	B-B5	K-B1
14	B-R7	K-K1
15	N-K5	K-B1
16	N-Q7ch	K-K1
17	K-K6	K-Q1
18	K-Q6	K-K1
19	B-N6ch!	K-Q1
20	B-R5	K-B1

211

21	N–B5	K–Q1
22	N–N7ch	K–B1
23	K–B6	K–N1
24	K–N6	K–B1
25	B–N4ch	K–N1
26	B–B5	K–R1
27	N–B5	K–N1
28	N–R6ch	K–R1
29	B–K4 mate	

212 *This is a check-mate position, as the Black King is in check and has no legal escape move. The checkmate process has two stages: driving the King to the edge of the board, and then to the corner where checkmate is administered.*

The mate must be executed with the weaker side's King *in a corner of the same color as those on which the Bishop travels.* The mating process here is really quite taxing even for a strong player; but luckily, this type of mate is rare.

Despite, or perhaps because of, its difficulty, the mate with Bishop and Knight deserves attentive study. Many great masters and teachers have strongly recommended repeated drill with this type of mate because of its instructive revelation of the cooperative power of the pieces. Hunting down the lone King has all the attraction of a suspense thriller!

When you first attempt to work out this mate, you will probably find your prey escaping you; exactitude will come with practice. About 30 moves is par for this mate; 50 moves is the limit!

TACTICAL FINE POINTS

CHESS is a game in which mastery of attack and defense is vital. It is important, therefore, to have a good understanding of exchanges, threats and tactical methods.

Exchanges

SUPERIORITY in material is one of the basic devices for winning a game. It is essential that you obtain good value for every bit of material you part with. Here are some useful examples:

213 1 *PxP*   *PxP*
Material is still even. Each player has won (and lost) a Pawn.

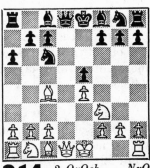

214 2 *QxQch*   *NxQ*
Now White wins a Pawn with 3 NxP. (If 2 . . . KxQ; 3 BxBP wins a Pawn.)

The improper way (Diagram 215) and the proper way (Diagram 216) to exchange:

215 1 NxP??   PxN
White has won a Pawn, but lost a Knight, which is of much greater value.

216 1 BxN   QPxB
White has parted with a Bishop, but won a Knight (even exchange).

Threats

THREATS are the means by which tactical ideas are executed. The strongest threats are those which hit two objectives simultaneously, or those which muster more force for attack than your opponent has for defense.

There is great variety in the techniques which may be used in setting up and executing threats. One of the most common is the *pin*, shown in Diagrams 217-222. The *Skewer* is shown in Diagram 220. Forks (double attacks) are also immensely useful as threats. These are illustrated in Diagrams 223-232 in fairly simple form.

217 1 B-KR6 P-KN3
*Black has no choice; mate is threatened, and his King Knight Pawn is pinned.**

218 2 BxR BxB
*White has won the exchange (winning a Rook in return for Bishop or Knight).***

219 1 B-K5 . . . .
This pins (and wins) the Black Queen in return for only a Bishop.

220 1 R-R8ch . . . .
This wins a whole Rook after the Black King walks out of check.

---

* Piece A is said to pin piece B when piece B cannot move for fear of exposing a more important piece to attack. If the King is the screened piece, then it would be illegal to move the pinned piece (*see Diagram 221*).

**As the Rook is more valuable than a Bishop or Knight, winning the exchange is a profitable transaction.

221 Black's Knight at QB3 is pinned, as it screens the Black King from attack by White's Bishop at QN5. It would therefore be illegal to move the Knight from QB3.

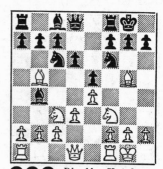

222 Black's Knight at KB3 is pinned, as it screens the Black Queen from attack by White's Bishop at KN5. To move the pinned Knight is legal but virtually unthinkable.†

223 Black plays ... Q-N3ch, attacking the Bishop as well.

224 White must get out of check; his Bishop is lost.

---

† Black cannot afford to lose his Queen for only a Bishop.

White's Queen at K4 threatens mate at KR7 and also threatens Black's Rook at QR1 (White's QR8). Black must stop the mate, thereby permitting the loss of his Rook.

225 *White plays Q–K3, attacking both Rooks, which are unprotected.*

226 *Black must lose a Rook; the Rooks cannot guard each other.*

Black's King protects Black's Queen. But White plays BxPch! forcing Black's King to give up the protection of his Queen. After 1 . . . KxB there follows 2 QxQ and White has won the Queen in return for only a Bishop.

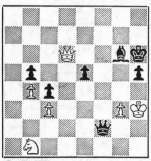

227 *Black cannot play . . . BxN because his Bishop is pinned. Instead, he plays . . . Q–B8ch.*

228 *White must move his King, after which Black continues . . . QxN, winning a piece.*

229 Black wins a piece by a neat combination of direct attack and "discovered" attack. The key move is ... PxP.

230 White's Queen is attacked, and at the same time his Knight at KN5 is menaced! If 2 BxBP, Bx Nch and 3 ... QxN.

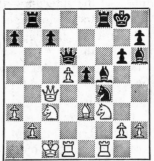

231 Black wins by an astonishing move: 1 ... Q–N3!!! threatening ... QxP mate and also attacking White's Bishop. Both threats cannot be parried, so White plays 2 BxQ. What now?

232 Now comes the even more amazing point of Black's remarkable Queen sacrifice: 2 ... N–K7 mate! This is a double check (see the Black Bishop at KR3?) and White's King is trapped.

The examples in Diagrams 217-232 give us a good idea of what can be accomplished by pins and double attacks. We shall now proceed to more complex forms of tactical play, which sometimes require as many as four diagrams for adequate explanation. Careful study of these examples will improve your play enormously and also enable you to get a great deal of fun out of chess.

Attack and Defense

IT is always fascinating to observe the interplay of attack and defense in chess. Alertness, foresight, accuracy all play their appointed roles. In Diagram 233 the Black pieces were played by the U. S. Champion, who nevertheless succumbed to an elementary stalemate stratagem. We may say "Elementary, my dear Watson" all we like, but the fact remains that nothing in chess is elementary in the sense that nothing can be taken for granted. True, principles and general rules must be accepted, but the important thing is to pierce to the heart of every position to find *the very best move,* be it ever so surprising.

233 White, who is three Pawns down, seems hopelessly lost. Yet he saves himself with 1 Q-KB2!!

234 As his Queen is now pinned, Black has no choice: he plays 1 ... QxQ, leaving White stalemated!

235 Would you believe that White has a forced mate in three moves? He begins: 1 R-R8ch, K-B2; 2 QxNch!!

236 Black's reply to this spectacular Queen sacrifice is forced: 2 ...KxQ. Now comes 3 R(R1)-R7 mate!

237 *Here is a really stunning example of the power of the pin. Again White has a forced mate in three, beginning with 1 R-R8ch!!, KxR; 2 Q-R6ch.*

238 *To his sorrow Black now realizes that he cannot capture White's Queen (see that White Bishop which has modestly retired to QR1?). So: 2 ... K-N1; 3 QxP mate.*

In the following positions we again see remarkable surprise moves. One of the most astonishing of the lot is undoubtedly the one that concludes the play in Diagrams 239-240. So simple, and yet far from easy to see! It takes imagination—and practice too—to see moves which are so simple and yet so deadly. The play in Diagrams 243-246 illustrates the same point: White's implacable will to attack turns up aggressive moves, which in turn lead to irresistible threats.

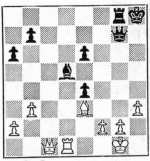

239 *Black threatens . . . QxP mate. Serious though the threat is, White need not worry, for he has 1 B-Q4!, P-K4 (the Queen is pinned); 2 BxP!! (another pin).*

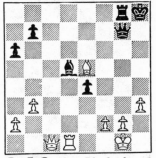

240 *Now Black plays 2 . . . QxB. Naturally he had no good alternative. Now we finally see the beautiful point of White's sacrifice: 3 Q-R6 mate! Black's Queen was too preoccupied!*

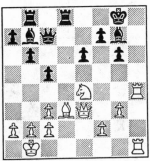

241 *An open King Rook file is always a menacing avenue of attack against a King castled Kingside. White proves this once more with 1 R-R8ch!!, BxR; 2 RxBch!, KxR.*

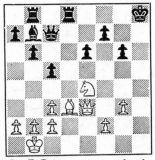

242 *Now we study the above position for the payoff: were White's sacrifices sound? Yes, for he continues 3 Q-R6ch, K-N1; 4 N-B6 mate. Black's King had no defensive support.*

243 *Black has three pieces for Queen and Pawn—an arithmetical plus for him (see p. 36). But White threatens BxR and also QxN (the King Pawn is pinned). So Black escapes with 1 . . . O-O.*

244 *Black's reply has been a clever one —or so it seems. Castling has killed two birds with one stone: Black's Rook is no longer attacked and the King Pawn is no longer pinned. But now White plays 2 Q-Q4.*

245 *White not only threatens 3 Q-N7 mate; he also attacks the Knight down at QR7. Black staves off mate by 3 . . . P-B3.*

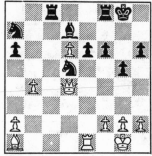

246 *True, Black has avoided mate; but now White carries out his other threat and plays 4 Qx N(R7). A good example of tactical play.*

247 *White plays a ridiculous-looking move: 1 QxR!, which is of course answered by 1 ... PxQ.*

248 *With 2 N-B6ch and 3 NxQ White proves the validity of his idea. The sacrifice leaves him a Rook up!*

249 *Black has a murderous discovered check: 1 ... P-K7ch. White's Rook at KB1 is attacked. He does not have much choice.*

250 *To save the attacked Rook, White "must" play 2 R-B2. But this allows 2 ... QxR(R8)ch winning.*

251 *A perfect setting for a discovered check turns up after 1 Qx Pch!!, BxQ.*

252 *Now White clears the vital diagonal with 2 P–B7ch, P–K4; 3 Bx P mate!*

253 *Here White has left his Queen Knight Pawn unguarded. At least that is what Black thinks, so he plays 1...QxNP???*

254 *However, the Queen Knight Pawn was only bait! There follows 2 N–QR4 and Black's Queen, is lost!*

255 *White plays the forking move 1 N-N6ch! despite the fact that Black can reply 1 ... PxN. What is White's idea?*

256 *White continues 2 PxNPch (a discovered check) and wins the Rook, as 2...R-B2 doesn't leave Black any better off.*

257 *White's method of winning a piece is simplicity itself and yet many players would overlook it: 1 P-KB3!, B-R4 and now 2 P-KB4!!*

258 *Now Black's Knight AND Bishop are attacked. If 2...BxB (what else?); 3 PxN wins a piece! Black's Bishop cannot move because his Queen is attacked!*

259 *White spurns Px N and finds a much more forcing line: 1 N–K7ch! (a double check!), K–R1; 2 N–N6ch!*

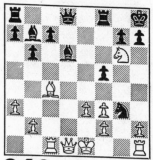

260 *Black must play 2 ...PxN, whereupon 3 RPxNch (a discovered check!) leads to quick mate!*

The range of difficulty in these positions is really amazing. For example, the fork in Diagram 261 is easy to see and anticipate; the fork in Diagram 255 was very hard to foresee. In other words, the *themes*, the *methods* repeat themselves endlessly; it is the application that differs, and here practice indeed makes perfect. As you progress, you will find that new positions echo old ones, that ideas you once used are susceptible of repeated use—always subject to caution: "does it still work?"

261 Black wins a piece by means of a fork: 1...N–R6ch is the necessary preliminary.

262 Now, wherever White plays, there follows 2...N–N4 attacking the Queen and winning the Bishop.

263 White can win the hostile Queen by force! 1 P–B7ch, K–R2 (1 ...B–N2 allows 2 P–B8 making a new Queen with check!); 2 Q–B5ch, K–R1; 3 Q–B6ch, K–R2.

264 White is now ready to win the Queen: 4 P–N6ch and Black's Queen is captured next move! This example is quite difficult and will repay careful study.

265 *See how White operates here with "windmill" checks: 1 R-N7ch, K-B1; 2 RxQPch (a discovered check), K-N1; 3 R-N7ch, K-B1. Poor Black's King has no choice but to wobble back and forth.*

266 *White has constructed the mating net: 4 R-QN7ch, K-N1 (he can't protect the Rook, as he must get out of check); 5 RxRch, N-B1; 6 RxN mate! Black's King was caught in a revolving door!*

In Diagram 267 and Diagram 269 we have delightful studies of a fascinating idea: discovered check to win the hostile Queen. When the idea of discovered check was first presented in simple form, it was not easy to see that the idea could take on such delightfully refined forms.

267 *Black sacrifices the Queen with 1 ...QxR! and after 2 RxQ, RxN; 3 RxR, RxR he has White on the ropes. White must not play 4 QxR as that would leave him a piece down.*

268 *Since 4 QxR won't do, White tries 4 Q-R3 (if 4 Q-N1, RxPch wins the Queen). But Black still wins the Queen: 4 ... RxPch; 5 K-R1, RxPch with discovered check AND attack on the Queen!*

269 *White has just offered his Queen for only a Knight. Black apparently considers this a blunder, for he calmly continues 1 ... PxQ. Now what? It would seem that the odds are overwhelmingly against White.*

270 *It is up to White to prove that his sacrifice of the Queen was correct. He plays 2 NxBch, and Black belatedly realizes that the situation is difficult. (If 2 . . . PxN; 3 R-N4ch, K-R1; 4 BxP mate!) The best is yet to come!*

271 *Becoming cautious, Black plays 2 . . . K-R1. But 3 R-R4! keeps up the surprise attack. (If 3 . . . PxN; 4 BxPch, K-N1; 5 R-N4 mate). So Black plays safe with 3 . . . P-KR3. If this "safe" move really worked, White's combination would be faulty.*

272 *Now an exquisite point is added to the Queen sacrifice: 4 Rx Pch!!, PxR; 5 N-K8ch (discovered check with attack on the Queen), K-R2; 6 NxQ and with a Bishop, Knight and Pawn for a Rook, White wins without much trouble. A brilliant conception!*

273 *White is strongly entrenched on the open Knight file, and he would like his Bishop to co-operate in striking at the vulnerable point KN7. He begins with an amazing move: 1 QxN!!—amazing but logical.*

274 *After 1 . . . QxQ; 2 P-QB4 is a puzzler. Black retreats his Queen—to avoid decisive material inferiority. Now we see White's idea: 2 . . . Q-Q2; 3 RxPch, K-R1; 4 R-N8ch!, KxR; 5 R-N1ch and mate next move.*

275 *White's play is intensely interesting because of the way that he forces the pace: 1 N-N6 (threatens to win a Rook), R-R2; 2 N(B3)xB, QxN (forced); 3 NxB, RxN.*

276 *Now White has the position for which he has been heading. The winning mechanism is a check which involves discovered attack: 4 BxPch winning the Black Rook at QB1!*

277 Black's pieces are huddled together on the Queen-side, but what of it? Just this: White can win a piece! He begins with 1 NxN, BxN; 2 Q-Q4! The drawback of Black's jumbled position is clear.

278 Two of Black's pieces are attacked. He tries 2 . . . B-R4; but then 3 P-QN4!, KR-Q1; 4 Q-B5 lays him low. Now three Black pieces are attacked! Loss of material is inevitable.

279 White is tremendously ahead in development. He strikes while the iron is hot: 1 BxP! Now he threatens B-K6ch or B-K8ch. Black's backward development deprives him of defensive resources.

280 Black is helpless against the threatened discovered checks; for if 1 . . . RxB; 2 Q-R8 mate; or 1 . . . QxB; 2 Q-Q8ch etc. White's lead in development made this sharp conclusion possible.

SURVEY OF
THE CHESS OPENINGS

SINCE about the beginning of the sixteenth century, chess theory has been the subject of intensive investigation. The bulk of this study has been devoted to the chess openings.

It is easy to see why this is so. A chess opening is a standardized series of moves for both sides at the beginning of the game. There is a great variety of openings and in the course of centuries their characteristics, merits and defects have become pretty familiar to students of chess theory. Despite the multiplicity of openings, their purpose is always the same: to assure one side, or the other, or both, that the best moves are being made at the beginning of the game. Since these opening moves will largely determine the trend of the coming play, it is clear that the first moves are of the greatest importance.

To attempt a study of the details at this stage, however, would be premature. Before you can know what to expect from the opening, you must know what you can expect from the rest of the game; you must know your preferences and tastes.

Hence all that is attempted here is to give you a nodding acquaintance with most of the openings that are still in use today. Some of them, like the Center Game, are hardly ever played. The Ruy Lopez, on the other hand, has enjoyed great popularity for a long time.

All the openings have *variations*—alternative possibilities which take on a sharply defined character differentiating them from other variations of the same opening. To give all these variations is beyond the scope of this book, and would in any event only confuse you. Hence one outstanding variation has generally been selected to give the "feel" of that line of play. Basic opening moves which give the opening its name appear in *italics*; the moves of the variation are given in regular type.

Center Game

THIS is rarely played nowadays because the early development of White's Queen involves loss of time.

WHITE	BLACK
1 *P-K4*	*P-K4*
2 *P-Q4*	PxP
3 QxP	N-QB3
4 Q-K3	N-B3
5 N-QB3	B-N5
6 B-Q2	O-O
7 O-O-O	R-K1

281 *Position after 7 ...R-K1.*

Black has an excellent development and a fine all-round position. It is therefore easy to understand why this opening is in disfavor.

Danish Gambit

HERE White offers the sacrifice of two Pawns in order to get a big lead in development.

WHITE	BLACK
1 P–K4	P–K4
2 P–Q4	PxP
3 P–QB3	PxP
4 B–QB4	PxP
5 BxP	N–KB3
6 P–K5	B–N5ch
7 N–B3	Q–K2
8 KN–K2	N–K5
9 O–O	. . . .

White has a formidable attack. He doesn't mind being several Pawns down!

282 Position after 9 O–O.

Scotch Game

ONCE quite popular, the Scotch is another line which is rarely seen nowadays.

WHITE	BLACK
1 P–K4	P–K4
2 N–KB3	N–QB3
3 P–Q4	PxP
4 NxP	N–B3
5 N–QB3	B–N5
6 NxN	NPxN
7 B–Q3	P–Q4
8 PxP	Q–K2ch!
9 Q–K2	NxP

Black has at least equality. Obviously the opening lacks sting.

283 Position after 9 ...NxP.

We are dealing here with openings in which both sides play 1 P-K4—probably best for the inexperienced player. We can already see even at this point that where White follows up with an early P-Q4, Black has no trouble getting an even game. P-Q4 requires more preparation.

Giuoco Piano

THEY call this the "quiet game" but there are times when it becomes wild and woolly!

WHITE	BLACK
1 P-K4	P-K4
2 N-KB3	N-QB3
3 B-B4	B-B4
4 P-Q3	N-B3
5 N-B3	P-Q3
6 B-K3	B-N3
7 Q-Q2	B-K3
8 B-N3	. . . .

284 Position after 8 B-N3.

This sedate line has little aggressive quality, but its placidity should recommend it to the beginner.

WHITE	BLACK
1 P-K4	P-K4
2 N-KB3	N-QB3
3 B-B4	B-B4
4 P-B3	N-B3
5 P-Q4	PxP
6 PxP	B-N5ch
7 N-B3	NxKP
8 O-O	. . . .

285 Position after 8 O-O.

Very wild this time! Even the masters are in doubt about the outcome. Ideal for skittles play.

Evans Gambit *

AN offshoot of the Giuoco Piano, this opening has produced some of the most brilliant games on record.

WHITE	BLACK
1 P–K4	P–K4
2 N–KB3	N–QB3
3 B–B4	B–B4
4 P–QN4	BxP
5 P–B3	B–R4
6 P–Q4	PxP
7 O–O	P–Q3
8 PxP	B–N3
9 N–B3	. . . .

White's splendid development gives him good attacking chances.

286 *Position after 9 N–B3.*

In the two variations of the Giuoco Piano given above, White either refrains from P-Q4, contenting himself with the more modest P-Q3—or else he prepares for P-Q4 by first playing P-QB3. Why do we say "prepares"? Because, in the event of a Pawn exchange in the center, White gets the "classical center"—two Pawns standing abreast on the fourth rank. This gives White a fine open game with good possibilities of development, and correspondingly takes away squares from Black's pieces in the center.

The Evans Gambit is an even more radical example of the same idea. White gives up a Pawn at an early stage in order to gain time to establish the "classical center."

---

* Openings which feature speculative sacrifices of material are known as gambits.

Two Knights' Defense

IF you want to avoid the Giuoco Piano or Evans Gambit, try the Two Knights' Defense:

WHITE	BLACK
1 *P–K4*	*P–K4*
2 *N–KB3*	*N–QB3*
3 *B–B4*	*N–B3*
4 *N–N5*	*P–Q4*
5 *PxP*	*N–QR4**
6 *B–N5ch*	*P–B3*
7 *PxP*	*PxP*
8 *B–K2*	*P–KR3*
9 *N–KB3*	*P–K5*

Black has a good initiative in return for the sacrificed Pawn.

287 *Position after 9 ... P–K5.*

By adopting the Max Lange Attack, White indicates at once that he seeks a vigorous attacking game. The Four Knights', on the other hand, is a slow-moving opening in which White refrains from an immediate P-Q4. The usual consequence is a heavy maneuvering game which requires a considerable store of patience.

---

* 5 ... NxP; 6 NxBP?!, KxN; 7 Q–B3ch, K–K3 is the famous "Fried Liver" Attack. It is unsound but very troublesome to play against.

Max Lange Attack

TRICKY and full of traps, this opening has puzzled the experts for decades!

WHITE	BLACK
1 P-K4	P-K4
2 N-KB3	N-QB3
3 B-B4	B-B4
4 O-O	N-B3
5 P-Q4	PxP
6 P-K5	P-Q4
7 PxN	PxB
8 R-K1ch	B-K3
9 N-N5	Q-Q4

After 10 N-QB3, Q-B4; 11 QN-K4, O-O-O the position is extremely complicated.

288 Position after 9 ...Q-Q4.

Four Knights' Game

PHLEGMATIC and solid, this opening appeals to the conservative-minded player.

WHITE	BLACK
1 P-K4	P-K4
2 N-KB3	N-QB3
3 N-B3	N-B3
4 B-N5	B-N5
5 O-O	O-O
6 P-Q3	BxN
7 PxB	P-Q3
8 B-N5	Q-K2
9 R-K1	N-Q1

White has two active Bishops, but Black's position is compact and safe enough.

289 Position after 9 ...N-Q1.

Ruy Lopez

FOR almost a century, the Ruy Lopez has been the favorite opening of those beginning with 1 P-K4. In most variations, it enables White to exert a pressure which is by no means easy to shake off.

WHITE	BLACK
1 P-K4	P-K4
2 N-KB3	N-QB3
3 B-N5	P-QR3
4 B-R4	N-B3
5 O-O	B-K2
6 R-K1	P-QN4
7 B-N3	P-Q3
8 P-B3	O-O
9 P-KR3	N-QR4
10 B-B2	P-B4
11 P-Q4	Q-B2
12 QN-Q2	. . . .

290 *Position after 12 QN-Q2.*

WHITE	BLACK
1 P-K4	P-K4
2 N-KB3	N-QB3
3 B-N5	P-QR3
4 B-R4	N-B3
5 O-O	NxP
6 P-Q4	P-QN4
7 B-N3	P-Q4
8 PxP	B-K3
9 P-B3	B-K2
10 B-K3	O-O
11 QN-Q2	NxN
12 QxN	. . . .

291 *Position after 12 QxN.*

The first variation (see Diagram 290) leads to complex maneuvering. The second variation (Diagram 291) leads to a more open game, with a lively battle in prospect.

In the first variation, the position will be congested for a long time and perhaps even for the whole duration of the game, leading to a type of play which requires considerable patience on the part of both players. The second variation is certainly more enterprising, but it has the drawback for Black that he is frequently subjected to a powerful attack after castling.

Petroff Defense

IF imitation is the sincerest form of flattery, then the Petroff is often very flattering!

WHITE	BLACK
1 *P–K4*	*P–K4*
2 *N–KB3*	*N–KB3*
3 NxP	P–Q3
4 N–KB3	NxP
5 Q–K2	Q–K2
6 P–Q3	N–KB3
7 B–N5	QxQch
8 BxQ	B–K2
9 N–B3	P–KR3
10 B–R4	B–Q2

The position is fairly level. White is more comfortable.

292 *Position after 10 ...B–Q2.*

Philidor Defense

CONGESTED positions are usually the curse of this defense, as far as Black is concerned.

	WHITE	BLACK
1	P–K4	P–K4
2	N–KB3	P–Q3
3	P–Q4	N–KB3
4	N–B3	QN–Q2
5	B–QB4	B–K2
6	O–O	O–O
7	Q–K2	P–B3
8	P–QR4	Q–B2
9	B–N3	P–KR3

Black will have great difficulty in completing his development properly.

293 *Position after 9 ... P–KR3.*

Vienna Game

PREPARING for the advance of his King Bishop Pawn is the keynote of White's play in this opening.

	WHITE	BLACK
1	P–K4	P–K4
2	N–QB3	N–KB3
3	P–B4	P–Q4
4	BPxP	NxP
5	N–B3	B–K2
6	P–Q4	O–O
7	B–Q3	P–KB4
8	PxP e.p.	BxP
9	O–O	N–B3

Black has a nice development and may expect to hold his own.

294 *Position after 9 ... N–B3.*

King's Gambit

COMPLICATIONS generally come thick and fast in this the most volatile of all the chess openings. A sample is the Muzio Gambit:

WHITE	BLACK
1 P–K4	P–K4
2 P–KB4	PxP
3 N–KB3	P–KN4
4 B–B4	P–N5
5 O–O	PxN
6 QxP	Q–B3
7 P–K5	QxP
8 P–Q3	B–R3
9 N–B3	N–K2

White has enough attack to compensate for the missing piece.

295 *Position after 9 ... N–K2.*

King's Gambit Declined

DISCRETION is the better part of valor: Black evades the complications of the gambit accepted.

WHITE	BLACK
1 P–K4	P–K4
2 P–KB4	B–B4
3 N–KB3*	P–Q3
4 N–B3	N–KB3
5 B–B4	N–B3
6 P–Q3	B–K3
7 B–N5	P–QR3
8 BxNch	PxB
9 P–B5	B–B1

White will advance his King-side Pawns; Black will aim for ... P–Q4.

296 *Position after 9 ... B–B1.*

* If 3 PxP??, Q–R5ch is murderous.

Falkbeer Counter Gambit

THIS is another— livelier—way to decline the King's Gambit. Enterprising players favor the Falkbeer.

WHITE	BLACK
1 *P–K4*	*P–K4*
2 *P–KB4*	*P–Q4*
3 KPxP	P–K5
4 P–Q3	N–KB3
5 PxP	NxKP
6 N–KB3	B–QB4
7 Q–K2	B–B4
8 N–B3	Q–K2
9 B–K3	BxB
10 QxB	. . . .

The ending after 10 . . . NxN is even.

297 *Position after 10 QxB.*

Sicilian Defense

BY adopting this complex but fascinating defense, Black avoids many of the standard lines resulting from 1 P-K4, P-K4.

WHITE	BLACK
1 *P–K4*	*P–QB4*
2 N–KB3	N–QB3
3 P–Q4	PxP
4 NxP	N–B3
5 N–QB3	P–Q3
6 B–K2	P–KN3
7 O–O	B–N2
8 N–N3	O–O
9 P–B4	B–K3

White has a strong hold on each of the important center squares.

298 *Position after 9 . . . B–K3.*

French Defense

MORE conservative than the Sicilian, the French is well-suited to the style of tenacious defensive players.

WHITE	BLACK
1 *P–K4*	*P–K3*
2 P–Q4	P–Q4
3 N–QB3	N–KB3
4 B–KN5	B–N5
5 P–K5	P–KR3
6 B–Q2	BxN
7 PxB	N–K5
8 Q–N4	P–KN3
9 B–Q3	NxB
10 KxN	P–QB4

A tense game of attack and counter-attack will follow.

300 Position after 10 ...P–QB4.

Caro-Kann Defense

ONE of the most phlegmatic lines at Black's disposal. It leads very frequently to a draw.

WHITE	BLACK
1 *P–K4*	*P–QB3*
2 P–Q4	P–Q4
3 N–QB3	PxP
4 NxP	B–B4
5 N–N3	B–N3
6 N–B3	N–Q2
7 P–KR4	P–KR3
8 B–Q3	BxB
9 QxB	Q–B2
10 B–Q2	KN–B3

White has only a slight initiative.

301 Position after 10 ...KN–B3.

In the three preceding diagrams, we have had examples of alternative replies to 1 P-K4. To the inexperienced player, such moves as 1...P-QB4 or 1...P-K3 or 1...P-QB3 may seem "evasive" or even "cowardly."

There are, however, several good reasons for sometimes varying from the tried and true 1...P-K4. For example, when your opponent makes a practice of playing 1 P-K4, he may be hankering to adopt a favorite line of play—one which he likes and one which makes you uncomfortable. To avoid such irksome variations, you may want to assert yourself by adopting a defense of your own choosing and liking.

Alekhine Defense

THIS is as lively and risky as the Caro-Kann is placid and safe!

WHITE	BLACK
1 *P-K4*	*N-KB3*
2 P-K5	N-Q4
3 P-QB4	N-N3
4 P-Q4	P-Q3
5 P-B4	PxP
6 BPxP	N-B3
7 B-K3	B-B4
8 N-QB3	P-K3
9 N-B3	Q-Q2
10 B-K2	O-O-O

White has somewhat the better of it.

302 *Position after 10 ...O-O-O.*

We come now to openings in which 1 P-Q4 is answered by 1 . . . P-Q4. As a rule, learners will find it advisable not to take up this opening too soon, as it requires some background of experience and familiarity with chess theory. The Queen Pawn. Openings are generally thought of as involving only positional problems. But these openings can also lead to brilliant King-side attacks, and in fact have produced the vast majority of brilliancy prize games in master play of the past forty years.

Queen's Gambit Accepted

BLACK's second move often allows White to get the whip hand in the center.

WHITE	BLACK
1 *P-Q4*	*P-Q4*
2 *P-QB4*	*PxP*
3 N-KB3	N-KB3
4 P-K3	P-K3
5 BxP	P-B4
6 O-O	N-B3
7 Q-K2	PxP
8 R-Q1	B-K2
9 PxP	O-O

Black's game is cramped, but he has good defensive possibilities.

303 *Position after 9 . . . O-O.*

Queen's Gambit Declined

THE great Tarrasch said of this opening that it is "the chamber music of chess." It is full of finesse.

WHITE	BLACK
1 *P-Q4*	*P-Q4*
2 *P-QB4*	*P-K3*
3 N-QB3	N-KB3
4 B-N5	QN-Q2
5 P-K3	B-K2
6 N-B3	O-O
7 R-B1	P-B3
8 B-Q3	PxP
9 BxBP	N-Q4
10 BxB	QxB

Black must still work hard to free himself.

304 *Position after 10 ...QxB.*

WHITE	BLACK
1 *P-Q4*	*P-Q4*
2 *P-QB4*	*P-K3*
3 N-QB3	N-KB3
4 B-N5	QN-Q2
5 P-K3	P-B3
6 N-B3	Q-R4
7 N-Q2	PxP
8 BxN	NxB
9 NxP	Q-B2
10 B-Q3	B-K2

White's position is freer; Black must be patient.

305 *Position after 10 ...B-K2.*

WHITE	BLACK
1 *P–Q4*	*P–Q4*
2 *P–QB4*	*P–QB3*
3 N–KB3	N–B3
4 N–B3	PxP
5 P–QR4	B–B4
6 P–K3	P–K3
7 BxP	B–QN5
8 O–O	O–O
9 Q–K2	B–N5
10 R–Q1	QN–Q2

White has more freedom.
Black is on the defensive.

306 *Position after 10 ...QN–Q2.*

WHITE	BLACK
1 *P–Q4*	*P–Q4*
2 *P–QB4*	*P–QB3*
3 N–KB3	N–B3
4 N–B3	P–K3
5 P–K3	QN–Q2
6 B–Q3	PxP
7 BxBP	P–QN4
8 B–Q3	P–QR3
9 P–K4	P–B4
10 P–K5	PxP
11 NxNP	....

A very complicated position!

307 *Position after 11 NxNP.*

Colle System

ONE of the best opening lines for inexperienced players. White's line of development is easy to master.

WHITE	BLACK
1 P–Q4	P–Q4
2 N–KB3	N–KB3
3 P–K3	P–K3
4 B–Q3	P–B4
5 P–B3	N–B3
6 QN–Q2	B–Q3
7 O–O	O–O
8 PxP	BxP
9 P–K4	Q–B2
10 Q–K2	. . . .

White's remaining problem is to develop the QB.

308 *Position after 10 Q–K2.*

This concludes our quick survey of the openings in which both sides play 1 P-Q4, P-Q4. One conclusion which deserves careful study on your part is that Black generally has trouble developing his Queen Bishop because its movements are blocked by the Black King Pawn at K3. (Note that this is not true of the variation illustrated in Diagram 306. Here Black defends with 2 . . . P-QB3, postponing . . . P-K3. This gives him a chance to play out the Queen Bishop and endow it with an active role.)

Aside from this point, you can appreciate from the last few diagrams how readily Black can get a terribly cramped position in this type of opening.

Nimzoindian Defense

THIS is a popular defense because it gives Black a chance to be enterprising as well as original.

WHITE	BLACK
1 P-Q4	N-KB3
2 P-QB4	P-K3
3 N-QB3	B-N5
4 Q-B2	N-B3
5 N-B3	P-Q3
6 P-QR3	BxNch
7 QxB	O-O
8 P-KN3	Q-K2
9 B-N2	P-K4

White for choice because his Bishops should have ample scope later on.

309 *Position after 9 ...P-K4.*

Queen's Indian Defense

BY adopting this defense, inexperienced players get a chance to experiment with the "fianchetto" (see Black's third and fourth moves and White's fourth and fifth moves).

WHITE	BLACK
1 P-Q4	N-KB3
2 P-QB4	P-K3
3 N-KB3	P-QN3
4 P-KN3	B-N2
5 B-N2	B-K2
6 O-O	O-O
7 N-B3	N-K5
8 Q-B2	NxN
9 QxN	B-K5

The position is about even. Note the great power of Black's Bishop at K5.

310 *Position after 9 ...B-K5.*

King's Indian Defense

STUBBORN and "hard-boiled," this defense is one that taxes the abilities of the greatest players.

WHITE	BLACK
1 P-Q4	N-KB3
2 P-QB4	P-KN3
3 N-QB3	B-N2
4 P-K4	P-Q3
5 P-KN3	QN-Q2
6 B-N2	0-0
7 KN-K2	P-K4
8 0-0	R-K1

White has slightly better control of the vital center squares, but Black has ample maneuvering space.

311 Position after 8 ...R-K1.

Gruenfeld Defense

HERE again the fianchetto plays a big role as Black tries to exert pressure against White's center Pawns.

WHITE	BLACK
1 P-Q4	N-KB3
2 P-QB4	P-KN3
3 N-QB3	P-Q4
4 PxP	NxP
5 P-K4	NxN
6 PxN	P-QB4
7 B-QB4	B-N2
8 N-K2	0-0

Black's "fianchettoed" Bishop plays a commanding role. Can White maintain his imposing center Pawns?

312 Position after 8 ...0-0.

Budapest Defense

"COUNTER-ATTACK" or "gambit" would be a more accurate term than "defense." The Budapest is favored by adventurous spirits.

WHITE	BLACK
1 P-Q4	N-KB3
2 P-QB4	P-K4
3 PxP	N-N5
4 B-B4	N-QB3
5 N-KB3	B-N5ch
6 QN-Q2	Q-K2
7 P-QR3	N(N5)xKP
8 NxN	NxN
9 P-K3*	BxNch
10 QxB	P-Q3

White's Bishops should have good play later on.

313 *Position after 10 ...P-Q3.*

The positions shown in Diagrams 309-314 illustrate some of the so-called "irregular" defenses against 1 P-Q4. These "irregular" moves serve the same purpose against 1 P-Q4 as the French, Sicilian and other defenses against 1 P-K4. Black is able to assert his own will, play the lines of his choice, steer the game into the channels he prefers. However, such defenses as the King's Indian or Budapest or Gruenfeld should not be ventured on without some previous preparation.

---

* If 9 PxB??, N-Q6 mate!

Dutch Defense

Although this is called a "defense" it is definitely aggressive in intent.

WHITE	BLACK
1 P–Q4	P–KB4
2 P–KN3	P–K3
3 B–N2	N–KB3
4 N–R3	P–Q4
5 P–QB4	P–B3
6 O–O	B–Q3
7 N–B3	O–O
8 Q–Q3	Q–K1

314 *Position after 8 ...QN–Q2.*

White's fianchettoed Bishop strikes powerfully along the long diagonal. Black has a "stonewall" formation.

Thus we conclude our brief survey of the openings. A few simple rules should be helpful:

1. Play out a center Pawn for your first move.

2. Unless some special point is involved, try to develop a piece on each of your early moves.

3. If it can be helped, try to avoid moving an already developed piece instead of a new piece.

4. Consider castling a developing move. Play it fairly early, to keep your King out of trouble.

INDEX

73 74   12 11 10 9 8 7 6 5